W9-BYZ-134

Preschool Art

Collage and Paper

MaryAnn F. Kohl
Illustrations: Katheryn Davis

Dedication

Dedicated in memory of my grandmother, Mary Geanne Faubion Wilson,
the first published author I ever knew, who sparked my imagination
when she told me that angels made my freckles
when they kissed me on the nose as I slept.

Acknowledgments

I would like to thank my editor, Kathy Charner, for her humor and kindness
in our editor-author relationship. Sometimes I think we have too much fun to call this work!
In addition, I would like to thank the owners of Gryphon House, Leah and Larry Rood,
for their support and friendship, and their belief in this book and in me.
Most important, my thanks go to my husband, Michael,
and my daughters, Hannah and Megan, who keep my mind clear,
tell me when I've been wonderful or when I haven't, and
remind me of what is most important in life.

A MARYANN KOHL BOOK   A MARYANN KOHL BOOK

Collage
and
Paper

It's the process, not the product!

MaryAnn F. Kohl

gryphon house®, inc.
Beltsville, Maryland

ALEXANDRIA LIBRARY
ALEXANDRIA, VA 22304

Copyright © 2001 MaryAnn F. Kohl
Published by Gryphon House, Inc.
10726 Tucker Street, Beltsville, MD 20705
Visit us on the web at www.gryphonhouse.com

All rights reserved. No part of this publication may be reproduced, stored in a retrieval system or transmitted in any form or by any means, electronic, mechanical, photocopying, recording or otherwise, without prior written permission of the publisher.

Library of Congress Cataloging-in-Publication Data

Kohl, MaryAnn F.,
     Preschool art: it's the process, not the product! / MaryAnn F. Kohl; [illustrations, Katheryn Davis].
          p.   cm.
     "A MaryAnn Kohl book."
     Inludes indexes.
     Contents: [1] Craft and construction --[2] Clay, dough, and sculpture -- [3] collage and paper -- [4]
     Painting -- [5] Drawing.
     ISBN 0-87659-252-3 (v.3)
     1. Art--Study and teaching (Preschool)--Handbooks, manuals, etc. I. Title: craft and construction. II. Title: Clay, dough, and sculpture. III. Title: Collage and paper. IV. Title: Painting. V. Title: Drawing. VI. Davis, Katheryn. VII. Title.
LB1140.5.A7 K64 2001
372.5'044--dc21

                                                                                              2001018468

Illustrations: Katheryn Davis
Cover photograph: Straight Shots Product Photography, Ellicott City, Maryland.

Bulk purchase

Gryphon House books are available at special discount when purchased in bulk for special premiums and sales promotions as well as for fund-raising use. Special editions or book excerpts also can be created to specification. For details, contact the Director of Marketing at the address above.

Disclaimer

The publisher and the author cannot be held responsible for injury, mishap, or damages incurred during the use of or because of the activities in this book. The author recommends appropriate and reasonable supervision at all times based on the age and capability of each child.

Table of Contents

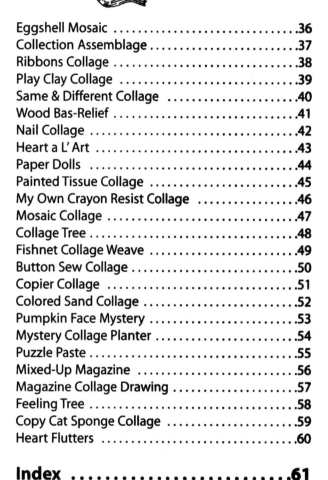

Introduction 6

Activities

It's the Process, Not the Product

Why is art process important?

Young children do art for the experience, the exploration, and the experimentation. In the "process" of doing art, they discover creativity, mystery, joy, and frustration, which are all important pieces in the puzzle of learning. Whatever the resulting masterpiece—be it a bright sticky glob or a gallery-worthy piece—it is only a result to the young child, not the reason for doing the art in the first place.

Art process allows children to explore, discover, and manipulate their worlds. Sometimes the process is sensory, such as feeling slippery cool paint on bare fingers. Other times it is the mystery of colors blending unexpectedly, or the surprise of seeing a realistic picture evolve from a random blob of paint. Art process can be a way to "get the wiggles out," or to smash a ball of clay instead of another child.

How can adults encourage the process of art?

Provide interesting materials. Stand back and watch. Offer help with unruly materials, but keep hands off children's work as much as possible. It's a good idea not to make samples for children to copy because this limits their possibilities.

Sometimes adults unknowingly communicate to a child that the product is the most important aspect of the child's art experience. The following comments and questions serve as examples of things to say that will help encourage each child to evaluate his or her own artwork:

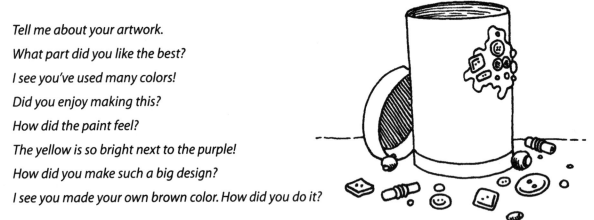

Tell me about your artwork.

What part did you like the best?

I see you've used many colors!

Did you enjoy making this?

How did the paint feel?

The yellow is so bright next to the purple!

How did you make such a big design?

I see you made your own brown color. How did you do it?

Process art is a wonder to behold. Watch the children discover their unique capabilities and the joy of creating. This is where they begin to feel good about art and to believe that mistakes can be a stepping stone instead of a roadblock in art as well as in other aspects of their lives. A concept children enjoy hearing is, "There's no right way, there's no wrong way, there's just your way."

Getting Ready!

Being prepared makes art experiences all the more enjoyable.
Here are some tips for success:

Covered Workspace

Cover the workspace—whether it is a table, floor, chair, wall, or countertop—with newspaper. Tape it down to prevent wiggles and spills of art materials. It's so much easier to bunch up sheets of paint-filled, sticky newspaper and find a clean space underneath than to clean up uncovered workspaces time and again. Other workspace coverings that work well are sheets of cardboard, an old shower curtain, a plastic tablecloth, big butcher paper, and roll ends of newsprint from the local newspaper print shop.

Handy Cleanup

Make cleanup easy and independent for young artists. All the less worry for the adult in charge! Place a wet sponge or pads of damp paper towels next to the art project for a simple way to wipe fingers as needed. Rather than have children running to the sink, fill a bucket with warm soapy water and place it next to the work area. Then add a few old towels for drying hands. Damp rags and sponges are handy for wiping spills, tidying up, and cleaning splatters as needed.

The Cover-up

Any old apron, Dad's old shirt (sleeves cut off), a smock, and a paint shirt are all helpful cover-ups for creative preschoolers. Instead, consider this: wear old play clothes and old shoes and call them "art clothes," used for art only. It's a wonderful feeling to get into art without being concerned about protecting clothing. These clothes become more unique with time and are often a source of pride!

Other Tips

- Create a separate drying area covered with newspapers. Allow wet projects to dry completely.
- Always protect a larger circle of space than the immediate area around the project. Think about floors, walls, and carpets (maybe even ceilings!).
- Shallow containers are often mentioned in the Materials lists. These include cookie sheets, flat baking pans, clean kitty litter trays, plastic cafeteria trays, painter's pans, and flat dishes and plates.
- It's never too late to start collecting recyclables for art. Save collage materials, fabric and paper scraps, Styrofoam grocery trays, yarn, sewing trims, and even junk mail. See pages 9 and 10 for a more comprehensive list of materials to save.
- Wash hands thoroughly before starting any edible activity.
- Do activities inside or out unless specifically noted as an outdoor activity only.

Using the Icons

Each page has icons that help make the projects in Paper and Collage more useable and accessible. The icons are suggestions only. Experiment with the materials, vary the suggested techniques, and modify the projects to suit the needs and abilities of each child.

Age

The age icon indicates the general age range of when a child can create and explore independently without much adult assistance. The "& Up" means that older children older will enjoy the project, and that younger children might need more assistance. Children do not always fit the standard developmental expectations of a particular age, so decide which projects suit individual children and their abilities and needs.

Planning and Preparation

The plan and prep icon indicates the degree of planning or preparation time an adult will need to collect materials, set up the activity, and supervise the activity. Icons shown indicate planning that is easy or short, medium or moderate, or long and more involved.

Help

The help icon indicates the child may need extra assistance with certain steps during the activity from an adult or even from another child.

Caution

The caution icon appears for activities that use materials that may be sharp, hot, or electrical in nature. These activities require extra supervision and care.

Hints

Hints are suggestions for the adults working with the artists.

Collage Materials List

A
acorns
allspice
almonds
aluminum foil
apple seeds
apricot seeds

B
ball bearing
balsa wood
bamboo
bamboo skewers
bark
basket reeds
beads
beans
belts
bias tape
bingo markers
blotter paper
bobby pins
bolts and nuts
bones
bottles
bottle caps
boxes
brads
braiding
broken parts
broken toys
buckles
burlap
burlap scraps
buttons

C
cancelled stamps
candles
candy
candy wrappers
cans
cardboard scraps
carpet samples
carpet wrap
cellophane
cellophane scraps
cellophane tape
chains
chalk
checkers
clock parts
clothespins
cloth scraps
cloves
coffee filters
coffee grounds
coins
comb
confetti
construction paper scraps
contact paper
cord
corks
corn, husks
corn, kernels
corn, kernels, dried
costume jewelry
cotton
cotton balls
craft eyes
craft sticks
crepe paper scraps
crystals

D
dice
dominoes
drapery samples
dried beans and peas
dried flowers
dried grass
dried seeds
driftwood
dry cereals

E
Easter grass
egg cartons
eggshells
eggs, plastic Easter
elastic
emery boards
embroidery floss
embroidery floss, hoops
erasers
evergreens
eyelets
excelsior

F
fabric
faucet washers
feathers
felt
felt scraps
film canisters
film cartridges
film spools
filters
fish tank gravel
fishing lures
flashbulbs
flocking
florist's foil, foam, tape
flowers
flowers, artificial
flowers, dried
flowers, plastic
form packing
fur samples

G
gauze
gift wrap
glass beads
glass mosaic pieces
glitter
gold costume jewelry
gold jewelry parts
gold thread
grains
gravel
greeting cards
gummed labels
gummed paper
   reinforcements
gummed paper

H
hair netting
hairpins
hair rollers
hardware items
hardware scraps
hat trimmings
hooks

I
ice cream sticks
inner tube scraps

J
jars
jewelry pieces
jewelry wire
junk of all kinds
jute

K
key rings
key tabs
keys

L
labels
lace
laminated items
leather
leather scraps
leaves
lentils
lids
linoleum scraps

M
macaroni
mailing tubes
map pins
marbles
masonite
meat trays
meat trays, paper
meat trays, plastic
meat trays, Styrofoam
metal scraps
metal shavings
mirrors
mosquito netting
moss, dried

N
nails
newspaper
noodles, dry
noodles, wet
nut cups
nuts

O
oilcloth scraps
orange seeds
orange sticks
origami paper
ornaments

P
paint chips
paper baking cups
paper cups
paper clips
paper dots
paper fasteners
paper products, all kinds
paper tubes
pebbles
pill bottles
pillboxes
pinecones
pine needles
ping-pong balls
pins, all kinds
pipe cleaners
pits from fruit
plastic, all kinds
plastic bottles
plastic foam
plastic scraps
popcorn
potatoes
pumpkin seeds

Q
Q-tips
quartz crystals
quills

R
raffia
recording tape
rhinestones
ribbon
rice
rickrack
rock salt
rocks
rope pieces
rubber bands
rubber tubing

S
safety pins
salt crystals
sandpaper
sawdust
scouring pads
screening, plastic or wire
screws
seals
seals, gummed
seam binding
seashells
seedpods
seeds
sequins
sewing tape
shoe laces
shot
silk scraps
skewers, bamboo
skewers, wooden
soap
soldering wire
spaghetti
sponges
spools
spray can lids
stamps, all kinds
stars, bummer
steel wool
sticks
sticky-dots
stones
straws, broom
straws, drinking
straws, stirring
string
Styrofoam

T
tape, all kinds
tape, cellophane
tape, library
tape, masking
tape, mystic
tape, plastic
tape, Scotch
tape, sewing
telephone wire
thistles
thread
tiles
tinker toy parts
tissue paper
tongue depressors
toothbrushes
toothpicks
torn paper scraps
twigs
twine

U
ukulele strings

V
velvet scraps
vermiculite

W
wallpaper
warp
washers
wax candles
weeds
wood scraps
wood shavings
wooden beads
wooden dowels
wooden wheels
wool
wrapping papers

X
X-rays

Y
yarn

Z
zippers

Collage

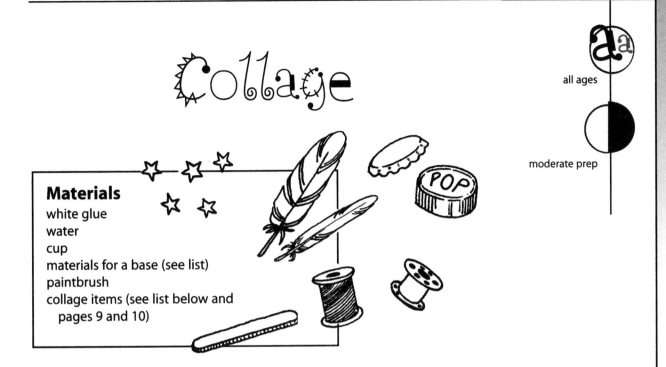

all ages

moderate prep

Materials
white glue
water
cup
materials for a base (see list)
paintbrush
collage items (see list below and
   pages 9 and 10)

Art Process
1. Mix white glue with water in a cup until it has a thin consistency.
2. Choose a base (see list) and place it on the work station.
3. Brush glue onto collage items (see list) and attach them to the base.
4. Make any design and use any amount or type of collage items to make it unique.
5. Allow the project to dry. If the glue is very thick, let it dry overnight.

Variations
- Use a large base and make a group collage project.
- Make a theme collage, such as shapes, colors, textures, foods, plants, or happiness.

Collage Items (Also see pages 9 and 10)

acorns	foil	pinecones
bark	gift wrap	ribbons
beads	glitter	rocks
bobby pins	gravel	sawdust
bolts	hair rollers	shells
bones	hooks	stars
bottle caps	ice cream sticks	sticks
cellophane	inner tube scraps	string
confetti	jewelry	telephone wire
cork	keys	tiles
cotton swabs	lace	toothpicks
eggshells	meat trays	wallpaper
embroidery thread	moss	wood scraps
fabric	newspapers	wood shavings
feathers	origami paper	wooden beads
felt	paper dots	yarn
flowers	pebbles	zippers

Materials for a Base
box
cardboard
matte board
old file folder
paper
paper plate
Styrofoam tray
wood

all ages

easy prep

help needed

Cut and Paste

Materials

scissors
scraps of colored paper, wallpaper, tissue paper,
   or magazine pages
paste or glue
paper

Art Process

1. Cut scraps of paper into any desired shape or design.
2. Paste or glue the shapes to a larger sheet of paper.
3. Continue cutting and pasting scraps of paper. Make random or realistic designs.

Variations

- Create a three-dimensional structure, sculpture, or construction.
- Make a theme Cut and Paste, such as Colors I Love, Wallpapers Only, My Happy Design, or Holidays.
- Add other collage items to the design.
- Tear the paper into shapes instead of cutting them with scissors.

Hint

- This activity is great for developing artists' creativity and fine motor skills.

Stick-On Stick-Upon

Materials

background or base materials (see list)
glue
cup
paintbrushes
masking tape, clear tape, or stapler
stickers
stick-on labels
collage items (see list on
   pages 9 and 10)

Art Process

1. Choose a background or base material (see list) and place it on the work-table.
2. Pour glue into a cup.
3. Glue, tape, staple, or stick collage items, such as cut-up scraps of paper, onto the base. Completely cover the base, if desired.

Variations

- Stick items onto a long piece of heavy yarn or rope and make a wild and crazy garland. Drape it around a room.
- Stick things onto yourself!

Hints

- Save a variety of stick-ons to repeat this activity over and over again.
- Limit the variety of stick-ons when beginning this project. Too many choices can confuse artists. As artists become more comfortable and creative, bring out more materials.

STICK THINGS
ON YOURSELF!

Background or Base Materials

cardboard boxes
large ice cream containers
newspaper
old posters or paper
plastic jugs

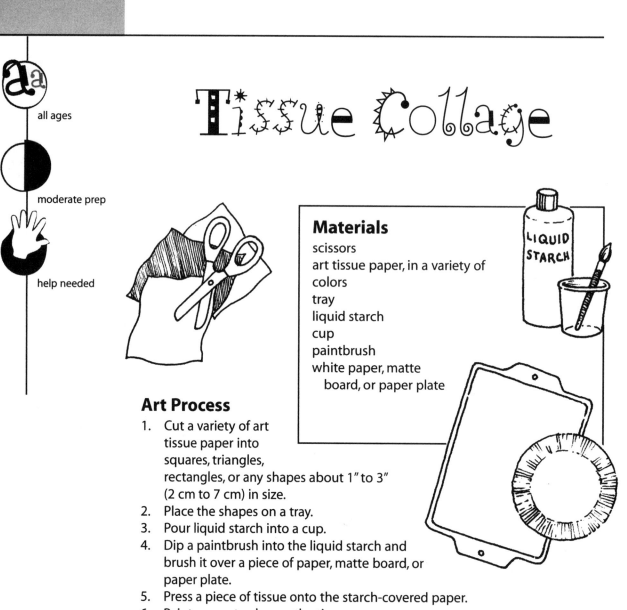

all ages

moderate prep

help needed

Tissue Collage

Materials

scissors
art tissue paper, in a variety of colors
tray
liquid starch
cup
paintbrush
white paper, matte board, or paper plate

Art Process

1. Cut a variety of art tissue paper into squares, triangles, rectangles, or any shapes about 1" to 3" (2 cm to 7 cm) in size.
2. Place the shapes on a tray.
3. Pour liquid starch into a cup.
4. Dip a paintbrush into the liquid starch and brush it over a piece of paper, matte board, or paper plate.
5. Press a piece of tissue onto the starch-covered paper.
6. Paint more starch over the tissue paper.
7. Continue adding more tissue paper and starch, overlapping them to create new colors. Cover all or part of the background paper.

ARRANGE TISSUE SHAPES ON TRAY

Variations

- Put tissue pieces onto wax paper, plastic wrap, or another type of background paper.
- Use clear contact paper and stick the tissue paper onto the sticky side of it without using starch. Then, cover the artwork with another piece of contact paper.
- Substitute thinned white glue for starch to make a stronger and glossier creation.

Hint

- Painting starch onto tissue causes the color or dye to drip from the paper. Although this creates a pretty effect, it can surprise some artists.

Easel Collage

Materials
large sheets of newsprint
easel, with clips
paint and paintbrushes
paper scraps (see list)

Art Process
1. Clip a large sheet of newsprint onto an easel.
2. Paint a picture on the newsprint.
3. Tear paper scraps (see list) into pieces and press them into the wet paint.
4. Let the papers show through, or paint over them.

Variation
• Press fabric scraps, magazine clippings, or photographs into wet paint.

Hints
• Place the small scraps of paper into cups or cans and put them in the easel tray next to the paints. Place larger scrap pieces into boxes on the floor next to the easel.
• Scissors are not necessary, but use them if desired. Hang scissors from a long piece of yarn attached to the top of the easel.

Paper Scraps
confetti
construction paper
facial tissues
old coloring book pages
stationary or note cards
tissue paper
wallpaper
wrapping paper

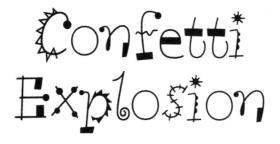

Confetti Explosion

Materials

white glue, in squeeze bottle
black paper
confetti, paper or metallic
    holes from paper
    punch

Art Process

1. Use glue to draw a design on a piece of black paper.
2. Sprinkle confetti and paper holes from a hole punch onto the glue design. Place confetti and dots on the glue one at a time or sprinkle it all at once.

Variations

- Use bits of tissue, cotton balls, beads, or other collage items instead of confetti.
- Fill a cookie pan about ¼" (6 mm) deep with confetti. Make a glue design on a piece of paper, turn it over, and press it into the confetti. Turn it right side up to dry.
- Place a glue design in the bottom of a tub of confetti. Scoop confetti over it, shake off the excess confetti, and allow it to dry.

Hints

- To place individual pieces of confetti onto the design, use a damp cotton swab to lift pieces of confetti and place them on the glue design.
- When creating a larger design, work on small parts at a time so the glue doesn't dry out.

Sticky Dot Collage

Materials

sticky dots, one color
contrasting color of
    paper

Art Process

1. Choose a color of sticky dots and a contrasting color of paper. (For example, sticking yellow dots onto purple paper is an effective illusionary combination.)
2. Stick a dot onto the piece of paper. Continue adding as many dots as desired, letting the contrasting paper show through between the dots.
3. When finished, stand back and look at the design.
4. For more optical fun, stare at the design for awhile, and then stare at a white wall. Can you see the dots?

Variations

• Cut a variety of colors of construction paper or colorful sticky-backed paper into squares, circles, and other shapes. Stick them onto a piece of background paper.
• Stick sticky dots on different kinds of backgrounds, such as small cards or even rocks!

Hints

• A good-sized paper to use is 8" x 10" (20 cm x 25 cm).
• Sticky dots create an optical geometric illusion when you place them on a paper of definite contrasting color, such as green dots on red paper, white dots on black paper, or purple dots on yellow paper. Look at a color wheel to see which colors are opposites and, therefore, most contrasting.

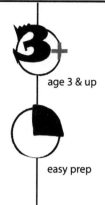

age 3 & up

easy prep

Yarn and String Collage

Materials
scraps of yarn and string
sewing trims and braids, optional
glue, tape, or stapler
paper or cardboard

Art Process
1. Sort through scraps of string and yarn and choose favorite pieces. Select sewing trims and braids too, if desired.
2. Glue, tape, or staple the scraps to a piece of paper or cardboard. Coil, twist, or fray the strands to provide a variety of design options.

Variations
• Use crayons or markers to color between the yarn and string shapes.
• Add paper scraps or other items from pages 9 and 10 to the collage.

Nature Collage

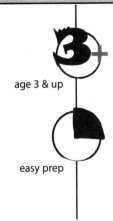

Materials

white glue
Styrofoam grocery tray
nature items (see list)
piece of wood
craft sticks or cotton swabs

Nature Items

bark
dried weeds
leaves
nuts
pebbles
pine needles
pinecones
seed pods
seeds
shells
wood shavngs

Art Process

1. Pour a puddle of glue into the middle of a Styrofoam grocery tray.
2. Select a nature item (see list) and arrange it on a piece of wood.
3. Dip a craft stick or cotton swab into the glue and brush it over the nature item. Or, dip the item directly into the puddle of glue.
4. Stick the item onto the piece of wood.
5. Add more nature items and glue them to the piece of wood.
6. Allow the collage to dry overnight or several days.

Variations

• Using markers or paint, color the piece of wood before gluing items to it.
• Cover the piece of wood with fabric before starting the project.
• Instead of using wood as a base, use a paper plate, cardboard, or plaster of Paris in a pie plate.

Hint

• Use a glue gun for immediate, strong, long-lasting results. This requires constant one-on-one supervision.

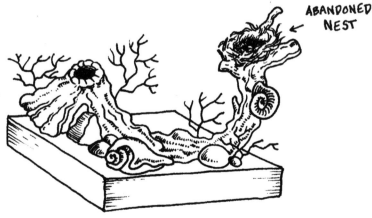

ABANDONED NEST

age 3 & up

easy prep

Feather Collage

Materials
feathers
glue
heavy paper or poster board
crayons or markers, optional

Art Process
1. Sort feathers according to size, shape, or color.
2. Glue feathers onto a piece of heavy paper, making a random design or a picture.
3. Allow the project to dry.
4. If desired, color the design with crayons or markers.

Variations
- Cover a bulletin board with bright paper and tack feathers onto it.
- To make a large Feather Design, cover a table with butcher paper. Sort feathers and any additional materials by size, shape, or color. A group of artists can assemble, glue, and tape materials and feathers to the large paper. After the design is dry, cover a wall or door with it.

Hints
- Bright feathers are available at craft stores.
- Feathers are versatile art materials. Artists enjoy them because they are soft and can be used to tickle friends!

Tissue Fingerpainting Collage

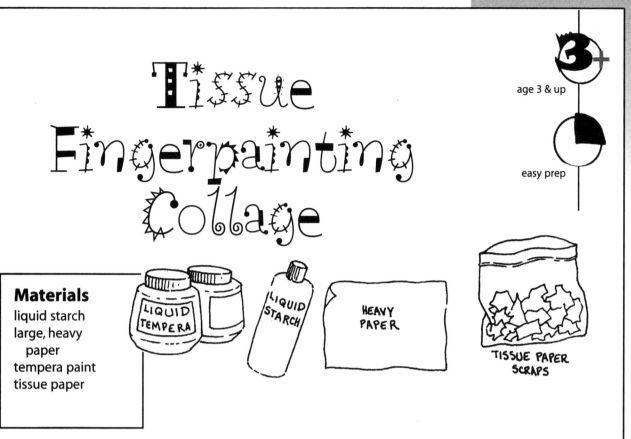

Materials
liquid starch
large, heavy
  paper
tempera paint
tissue paper

LIQUID TEMPERA

LIQUID STARCH

HEAVY PAPER

TISSUE PAPER SCRAPS

Art Process
1. Pour a puddle of liquid starch onto a large sheet of paper.
2. Sprinkle or pour tempera paint into the puddle.
3. Mix and spread the paint and starch over the paper to cover it.
4. Fingerpaint. Drag your fingers and fingernails through the paint to make designs.
5. Rinse and dry your hands.
6. Tear bright art tissue into large or small scraps.
7. While the paint is still very wet, press tissue scraps into it.
8. Allow the fingerpainting collage to dry.

Variations
- Sprinkle glitter, confetti, or other small scraps into the wet paint.
  - Cut cereal boxes or other cardboard containers into pieces and press them into the wet paint.

STARCH

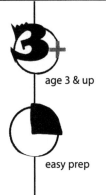

3+

age 3 & up

easy prep

Collection Collage

Materials
white glue
cups
collection of collage materials (see list below
    and on pages 9 and 10)
brushes
matte board, cardboard, wood, or heavy paper

Art Process
1. Pour glue into cups.
2. Glue an assortment of collage materials onto a piece of matte board, cardboard, wood, or heavy paper.
3. Dip a brush into the cup of glue and paint over the background surface.
4. Choose objects and place them onto the glue-covered background. Add additional glue if necessary.
5. Form a realistic picture or a random design.

Collage Materials
brads
crepe paper
fabrics
feathers
foil
magazine pages
notions
paper muffin cups
pipe cleaners
yarn

Variation
- Limit choices of material. For example, choose one decorating material and one interesting background material, such as feathers on wallpaper, pom-poms on colorful fabric, or yarn scraps on bright matte board.

String Collage

Materials

scissors
colorful yarn, embroidery floss, or string
liquid starch
Styrofoam tray
heavy paper

SOAK STRING IN
LIQUID STARCH.

Art Process

1. Cut string or yarn into 2' (0.5 m) lengths.
2. Pour liquid starch into a Styrofoam tray. Place the tray near the edge of a sheet of heavy paper.
3. Place the string into the starch and soak it for a few minutes.
4. Remove a strand of string from the tray and arrange it on the paper in any shape or design.
5. Repeat the process using many strands of different colored string.
6. Allow the String Collage to dry overnight.

Variation

• Place a strand of starch-soaked yarn onto a finger painting. Move it around in the painting to form designs.

Hint

• Substitute thinned white glue for starch—it works just as well.

Colored Toothpick Design

Materials
box of colored toothpicks
large tray, optional
white glue
construction paper or other heavy paper

Art Process
1. Dump toothpicks onto a table or into a large tray. (Be careful of the pointed ends.)
2. Sort the toothpicks according to color, if desired.
3. Glue toothpicks onto a piece of construction paper, making a design or picture.

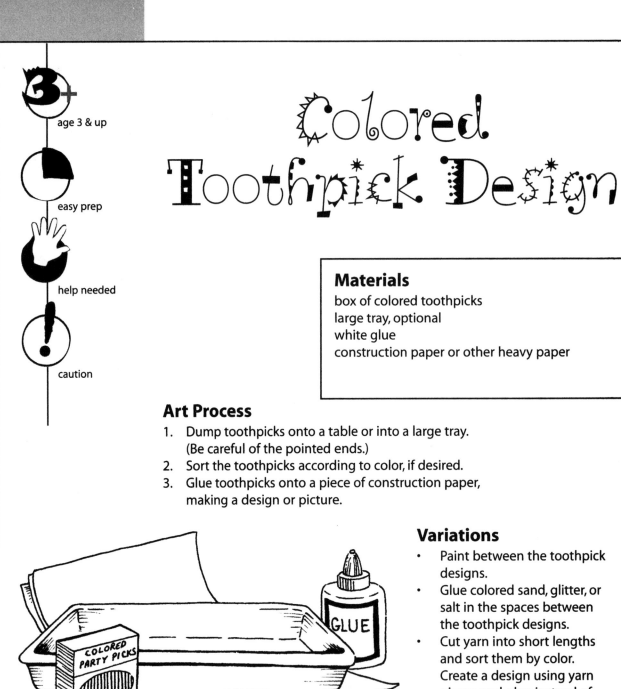

Variations
- Paint between the toothpick designs.
- Glue colored sand, glitter, or salt in the spaces between the toothpick designs.
- Cut yarn into short lengths and sort them by color. Create a design using yarn pieces and glue instead of toothpicks.
- Glue other materials, such as squares of paper, stickers, or beads, onto the toothpick designs.

Hint
- Young artists need some dexterity and eye-hand coordination to work with toothpicks. This is a new experience for most young artists and they can create some intriguing designs.

Leaf Collage

Materials

supple leaves, in assorted shapes and
   sizes
newspaper
white glue
poster board or matte board
crayons and markers, optional
clear plastic wrap
tape

Art Process

1. Collect fresh leaves in the spring or summer, or supple leaves in autumn.
2. Spread out the collection of leaves on a large sheet of newspaper.
3. Glue the leaves onto a poster board or matte board in any design.
4. Use crayons and markers to decorate the leaf collage, if desired.
5. Allow the project to dry overnight. (Leaves and glue take awhile
   to dry).
6. To save and protect the Leaf Collage, stretch a piece of clear plastic wrap
   over it and tape it to the back of the poster board.

Variations

- Place leaves between layers of wax paper, cover
  with newspaper, and iron with a warm iron.
  Ironing will seal the leaves between the sheets of
  wax paper. Display the creations in a window to see
  the "stained glass" effect and silhouettes
  of the leaves.
- Cut paper leaf shapes from wallpaper, wrapping paper, old
  posters, or other papers. Follow
  the same directions as for real
  leaves.

Hint

- One of the nicest things about working with leaves is
  that they are free and easy to find and collect, whether
  fresh and green in summer and spring or supple and
  colorful in autumn.

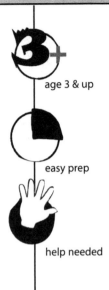

age 3 & up

easy prep

help needed

Tissue Contact

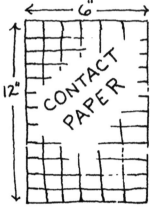

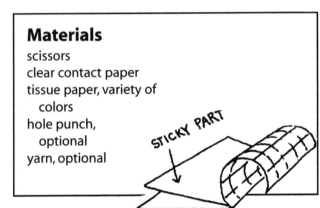

Materials

scissors
clear contact paper
tissue paper, variety of
  colors
hole punch,
  optional
yarn, optional

STICKY PART

Art Process

1. Cut a piece of clear contact paper into a 6" x 12" (15 cm x 30 cm) rectangle.
2. Fold the rectangle in half. Peel the backing halfway off the back, stopping at the fold.
3. Place the contact paper on a table, sticky side up.
4. Cut or tear tissue paper into small pieces and attach them to the sticky contact paper.
5. When finished, pull off the remainder of the contact paper backing, fold it over the remaining contact paper, and stick it to the design.
6. Trim off the ragged edges of the design.
7. If desired, punch a hole into the top of the design, tie a piece of yarn through it, and hang it in a window or near a light source.

Variation

- Cut the finished contact paper design into holiday shapes, such as hearts, dreidels, shamrocks, eggs, flags, or turkeys.

Hint

- Artists may find it difficult to fold contact paper, so it may be very wrinkly and off-center.

REMOVE ALL THE BACKING PAPER...

FOLD OVER

TRIM A SHAPE!

Scrap Match Collage

age 3 & up

easy prep

help needed

Materials

scissors
scraps of wrapping paper, several
  patterns
glue
cardboard
things to wrap (see list)

Art Process

1. Cut or tear a piece of wrapping paper into a design.
2. Glue the wrapping paper to a cardboard base.
3. Cut or tear another piece of wrapping paper into a different design. Glue it to the cardboard base.
4. Continue gluing different scraps of wrapping paper to the cardboard, covering it completely.
5. Wrap little toys, rocks, or other small items with the remaining scraps of wrapping paper.
6. Glue the wrapped items to the cardboard, matching together patterns of paper.

Things to Wrap

blocks
bottle caps
pieces of toys
small boxes
small rocks
small scraps of wood

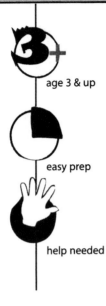

age 3 & up

easy prep

help needed

Paint Dough Collage

Art Process

1. Cut or tear interesting papers (see list) as desired.
2. Glue or tape the papers to a piece of matte board in any design, overlapping the papers. It is not necessary to glue down each edge of each scrap. (Covering the entire matte board is effective, but not required.)
3. Mix equal parts of flour, salt, and water in a bowl to form a paste consistency. Add paint and make as many colors as desired.
4. Fill squeeze bottles with the different colored mixtures.
5. Squeeze the mixtures onto designs around the collage pieces. Squeeze along the edges of the paper pieces to hold them down, if desired.

Materials

paper for the
   collage (see list)
scissors
glue or tape
matte board or
   poster board
measuring cup
flour
water
salt
bowls and spoons
tempera or water-
   color paint
plastic squeeze
bottles

MIX TO A PASTE CONSISTENCY,
THEN ADD PAINT!

Paper for the Collage

greeting cards
magazine pictures
newspaper
photographs
wallpaper
wrapping paper

Hints

- Salt gives the mixture a sparkling effect.
- When the mixture dries, it will be puffy and thick.

Sprinkle Collage

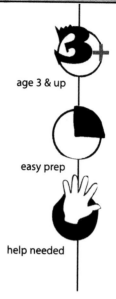

Materials

paper
tray or container
white glue in a squeeze bottle
sprinkles, such as glitter, confetti, seeds,
  or pine needles

Art Process

1. Place a piece of paper into a tray or container.
2. Squeeze white glue onto the paper to make a glue design.
3. Scatter sprinkles, such as glitter or confetti, over the wet glue design.
4. Curve the ends of the paper, carefully lift it from the tray, and dump the excess sprinkles into another tray or container. Reuse these sprinkles for another sprinkle design.

Variation

- Use other materials for sprinkling, such as wood shavings, sawdust, salt, powdered tempera, sand, or bits of yarn.

Hints

- Pour white glue into a squeeze bottle if it isn't already in one. Young artists, however, may find it easier to dribble glue from a stick or straw rather than controlling a squeeze bottle.
- Pouring or dumping excess sprinkles may be tricky for young artists, but offer assistance only if necessary.

age 3 & up

easy prep

help needed

Aromatic Pattern Collage

Art Process

1. Draw a design on a piece of paper using markers.
2. Pour glue into a cup. Add water to the glue until it has a runny consistency.
3. Dip a paintbrush into the glue and paint over a small section of the drawing.
4. Shake a spice (see list) over the glued section. Lift the paper and shake the excess spice into a flat pan (save it for other art projects).
5. Repeat the process on other sections of the paper to form a pattern of scents and aromas.
6. Allow the collage to dry. Hang it low enough on a wall so that everyone can enjoy the aromas at any time.

Variation

• Plan the sections of spices ahead of time. Then, draw patterns with the markers and glue spices over the patterns.

Materials

paper
markers
white glue
cup
water
paintbrush
spices, in shakers (see list)
flat pan

Spices

basil
cinnamon
cloves
ginger
mint
nutmeg
oregano
sage
thyme

ADD WATER UNTIL GLUE IS RUNNY...

PAINT A SMALL SECTION AT A TIME!

Button Box

Materials

colored paper
crayons, markers, paints, pencils, and other drawing
   tools
empty cardboard boxes
tape or white glue
buttons
collage items (see list)

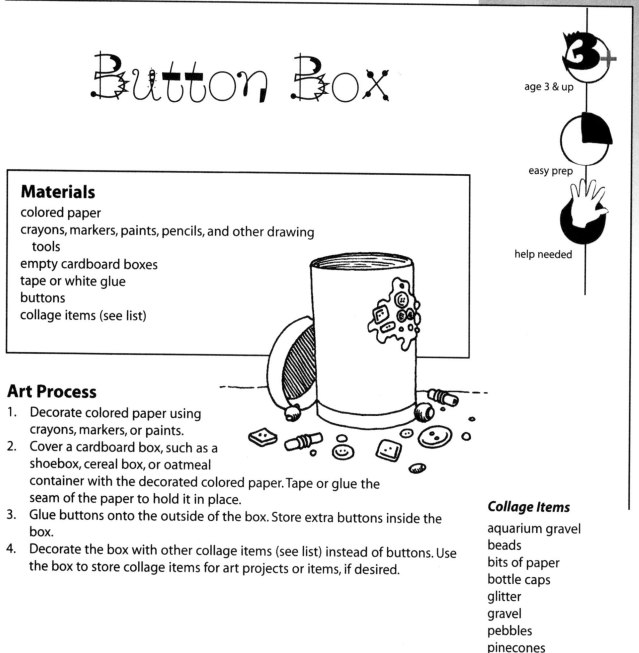

Art Process

1. Decorate colored paper using
    crayons, markers, or paints.
2. Cover a cardboard box, such as a
    shoebox, cereal box, or oatmeal
    container with the decorated colored paper. Tape or glue the
    seam of the paper to hold it in place.
3. Glue buttons onto the outside of the box. Store extra buttons inside the
    box.
4. Decorate the box with other collage items (see list) instead of buttons. Use
    the box to store collage items for art projects or items, if desired.

Collage Items

aquarium gravel
beads
bits of paper
bottle caps
glitter
gravel
pebbles
pinecones
scraps
shells
yarn

age 3 & up

easy prep

help needed

Bottle Cap Treasures

Art Process

1. Glue caps or lids to a piece of cardboard, with the opening of the cap or lid facing up.
2. Completely cover the cardboard with bottle caps or jar lids.
3. Choose "treasures" to glue inside the caps or lids. Glue one treasure into each cap.
4. Allow the Bottle Cap Treasure Collage to dry overnight.

Materials
white glue
caps and lids
   (see list)
cardboard
treasures (see list)

Variations

- Decorate the edges of the caps or lids using glitter and glue.
- Cover the cardboard with fancy wrapping paper before gluing the lids and treasures onto it.
- Paint the cardboard, allow it to dry, and glue lids and treasures to it.

Cap and Lid Sources

film canisters
juice bottles
mayonnaise jars
peanut butter jars
pill bottles
plastic milk jugs
soda bottles
spice jars

Treasures

beads
collected items
dried flowers
marbles
paint chips
photos
small drawings
small magazine
   pictures
stickers

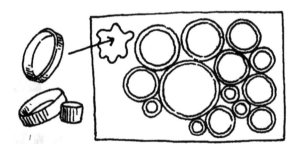

Pennies Collage

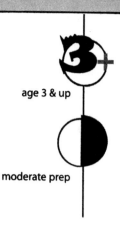

Materials
pennies
magnifying glass
masking tape
poster
board

Art Process

1. Spread out a handful of pennies on a table.
2. Explore the differences between the fronts and backs of the coins. Use a magnifying glass to see the details more clearly.
3. Put loops of masking tape onto one side of each penny.
4. Press and stick the pennies onto a piece of poster board. Place pennies head-side up or tail-side up in any design.
5. Enjoy the shiny pennies creation for as long as desired. Then, remove the pennies from the poster board and save, spend, or collect them.

POSTER BOARD

Variations

- Polish the pennies with a vinegar and salt mixture before using them to make them bright and shiny.
- Use both dull and shiny pennies and compare distinguishing characteristics.
- Substitute bottle caps or Legos for pennies.
- Draw and design around the pennies using markers or paint.
- Use other types of coins, including foreign or tourist coins.

Fun Shape Variety Base

Art Process

1. Draw a shape on a piece of heavy paper. Cut out the shape to form the base of the collage. Let the shape of the collage base inspire and challenge your creativity. Some examples of different shaped collage bases are:
   - letters or numerals
   - geometric shapes (circle, square, rectangle, triangle, trapezoid)
   - holidays (heart, flower, Christmas tree, star, birthday cake, pumpkin, egg)
   - animals (dog, dinosaur, mouse, bunny)
   - bugs (butterfly, caterpillar, bee, mosquito)
   - negative space (Cut out any shape from a piece of paper. The hole remaining in the paper is the negative space.)
2. Glue items onto the shape. Some fun collage ideas to go with a variety of bases are:
   - bunny shape with cotton balls
   - heart shape with red stickers
   - butterfly shape with colorful art tissue scraps
   - letter shape with items starting with that letter
   - numeral shape (such as a 6) with that many collage items
   - bird shape with birdseed
   - leaf shape with leaves, weeds, and flowers
   - flower shape with blossoms and torn grass bits

Materials
crayon or pencil
heavy paper
scissors
glue

Nail Board Collage

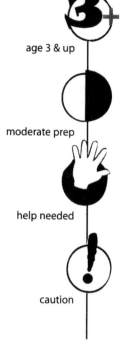
Materials

safety glasses
hammer
nails
plywood scrap or square
collage materials (see list on pages 9 and 10)
glue, string, or tape

Art Process

1. Put on a pair of safety glasses.
2. Hammer nails in any fashion into a scrap of plywood. Be careful not to hammer nails through the wood into a tabletop or floor.
3. When the nails are securely in place, decorate each nail with one collage material. Glue, tie, press, or attach them in any way.
4. Save the decorated sculpture, or remove the decorations and reuse the board to make a new collage.

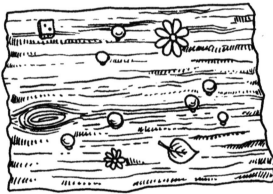

SIDE VIEW

Variations

- Glue beads or sequins onto each nail to make a sparkly collage. (Add some to the wooden base, too.)
- Stick toothpicks or bamboo skewers into a Styrofoam block and add decorative materials to each stick.
- Make a food collage by placing one bite of food onto each toothpick. Yummy examples are cubes of cheese or turkey, strawberries, chunks of pineapple, grapes, or banana slices. Serve and eat!

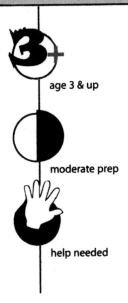

age 3 & up

moderate prep

help needed

Eggshell Mosaic

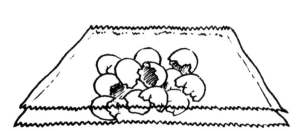

Materials
dyed eggs
wax paper
rolling pin
glue
matte board or
  cardboard

Art Process

1. Peel dyed eggs, such as those used at Easter. Save the eggshells until ready to use.
2. Place the eggshells on a piece of wax paper. Put another sheet of wax paper over the eggshells.
3. Roll a rolling pin over the wax paper to crush the eggshells.
4. Glue crushed eggshells onto a piece of matte board or cardboard.

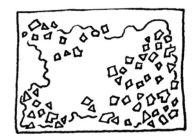

Variations

• Instead of dyeing eggs, color the shells of hard-boiled eggs using markers.
• Glue the pieces of eggshell into a definite mosaic pattern on a piece of heavy board or paper.
• Use tiny scraps of paper, confetti, or paper punch holes in addition to the eggshells.

Hint

• Young artists may not have the coordination or patience to pick up tiny pieces of shells. Young artists can dip a toothpick or cotton swab into the glue and then pick up a shell piece with it. Placing a small dot of glue on the paper will help artists deposit the shell onto the paper.

Collection Assemblage

3+

age 3 & up

moderate prep

help needed

Materials

materials for the assemblage (see list)
white glue, tape, paper clips, paper fasteners, yarn,
    or string
paints and brushes, optional

Art Process

1. An assemblage is a three-dimensional collage, made up of a diverse selection of materials.
2. Build, assemble, and attach objects (see list) to each other using tape, glue, paper clips, or string to make an assemblage design.
3. Allow the project to dry completely.
4. Decorate or paint the project, if desired.

Variations

- Feature a theme in the assemblage, such as Happiness, Spring, Robots, Space, or Transportation.
- Use only one kind of material for the assemblage, such as boxes, paper strips, wood scraps, or newspaper rolls.

Hint

- Use a glue gun for a quick-drying alternative to white glue. Supervise closely.

Materials for the Assemblage

acorns
berry baskets
colored wire
egg cartons
gift boxes
hole punches
pipe cleaners
pizza plates
spools
toilet tissue roll
wrapping paper

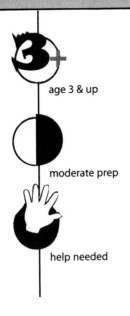

age 3 & up

moderate prep

help needed

Ribbons Collage

WHITE GLUE

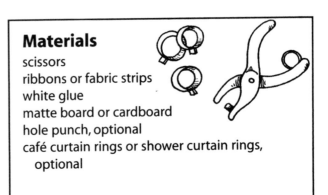

Materials

scissors
ribbons or fabric strips
white glue
matte board or cardboard
hole punch, optional
café curtain rings or shower curtain rings,
    optional

Art Process

1. Cut ribbons or fabric strips into manageable lengths.
2. Place glue on a strip of ribbon and glue it flat onto a piece of cardboard.
3. Continue gluing ribbon pieces in any pattern or design. Glue them side-by-side or cross them over each other.
4. Allow the project to dry completely.
5. If desired, punch two or more holes across one edge of the cardboard. Insert the curtain rings, one into each hole.
6. Hang the design on a stick or dowel, or tie ribbons to the rings and hang it anywhere.

Variations

- Bend, curl, or snip the ribbon to create a different look.
- Use sewing trims or scraps of wrapping paper.

Play Clay Collage

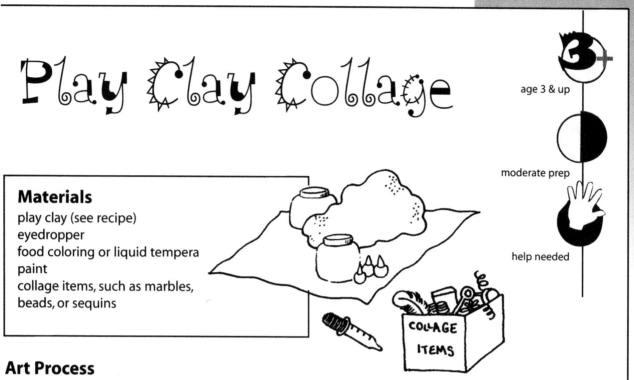

Materials

play clay (see recipe)
eyedropper
food coloring or liquid tempera paint
collage items, such as marbles, beads, or sequins

Art Process

1. Make Play Clay (see recipe). Knead it until it is smooth and soft.
2. Pull a small ball of clay from the larger ball. Squeeze a few drops of food coloring or paint onto it. Knead the color into the clay.
3. Pull more balls from the clay and mix color into them, too.
4. Form the balls of clay into any desired shape, joining and mixing different colors of clay balls into one design. (Flat shapes work best, but make other shapes as desired).
5. Press collage materials, such as sequins, beads, or marbles, into the Play Clay while it is still wet, forming any design or pattern.
6. Allow flat collages to dry for 24 to 48 hours. Thicker collages will take longer to dry.

Variations

- Instead of coloring the clay beforehand, use uncolored clay and paint it when dry.
- Make mosaic-like pictures in the clay.
- Write words or names using collage items.

Play Clay Recipe

measuring cups
flour
salt
warm water
bowl

Mix 4 cups (500 g) flour, 1 cup (250 g) salt, and 1 ¾ cups (420 ml) warm water in a bowl. Knead the mixture for about 10 minutes.

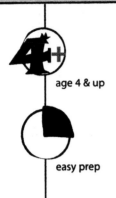

Same & Different Collage

Materials
paper plate
collage items
   (see list on pages
   9 and 10)
scraps of paper
white glue

Art Process
1. Fold a paper plate in half to form the base of the collage. Unfold it and set it aside.
2. Sort collage items into two piles: things that are alike and things that are different. The sorting possibilities are endless. Some examples are:
     • all buttons in one pile, everything else in the other pile
     • soft materials in one pile, hard materials in the other pile
     • red things in one pile, other colors in the other pile
3. Glue all or some of one kind of collage items onto one side of the paper plate.
4. Glue all or some of the other kind of collage items onto the other side of the plate.

Variation
• Tie sorted items onto a piece of string or yarn and hang it on a hoop or clothes hanger. Suspend it from the ceiling to create a "same and different" mobile.

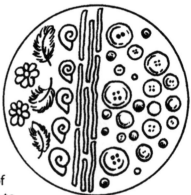

Hint
• Sorting materials into a pile of things that are the same and things that are different is one of the most basic levels of sorting. This collage project allows artists to record their sorting as well as create an interesting work of art.

Wood Bas-Relief

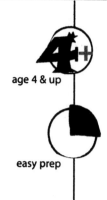

Materials

masonite or thin plywood
wood scraps
white glue
paints and brushes, optional

Art Process

1. Place a piece of masonite or thin plywood on the floor.
2. Attach wood scraps flat against the masonite using glue.
3. Allow the project to dry overnight.
4. Paint the bas-relief, if desired.

Variations

• Glue thick yarn into the relief between the wood scraps.
• Use thinned glue to attach magazine pictures, wrapping paper, or other paper to the pieces of wood.

Hints

• Good sources for wood scraps include framing shops, high school shop classes, cabinet shops, and construction sites.
• Use a glue gun for rapid attaching. Supervise closely.

Nail Collage

Materials
pencil
square of thick plywood
safety glasses
hammer
nails of all lengths and sizes, with and without
   heads
decorative items, such as yarn, beads, ribbons,
   and rubber bands

Art Process
1. Using a pencil, draw a simple design or object on a square of thick plywood.
2. Put on a pair of safety glasses.
3. Hammer one kind of nail into the penciled design. Try to keep the nails the same height.
4. Select another type of nail and hammer these into a different part of the design, keeping them about the same height, too.
5. Repeat the process using other types of nails.
6. If desired, add decorations, such as yarn, beads, ribbons, or rubber bands, to the design and secure them among the nails.

Variations
- Hammer nails into a board and use rubber bands to make designs.
- String embroidery floss from nail to nail to create a spider web effect.
- Cover the plywood with glued magazine pictures, paint, wrapping paper, or tissue paper before adding nails.

Hints
- To create texture on the shape, vary the height of the nails. For example, when designing a tropical fish, keep some nails low to form the outside shape, use large-headed nails to make scales and small-headed nails to make fins, and add string and yarn to provide color.
- Beginning artists often make random designs rather than realistic shapes.

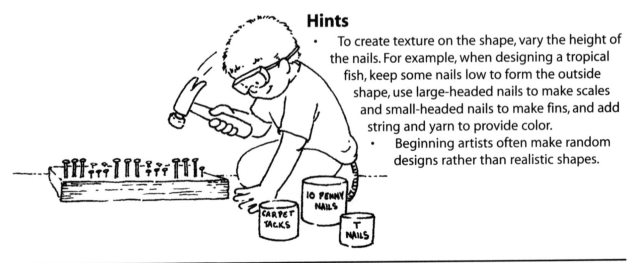

Heart a L' Art

Materials

heart-shaped stencils
  or patterns
papers (see list)
pencil
scissors
glue
matte board or cardboard
crayons, markers, paints, or any
  drawing/coloring tools, optional

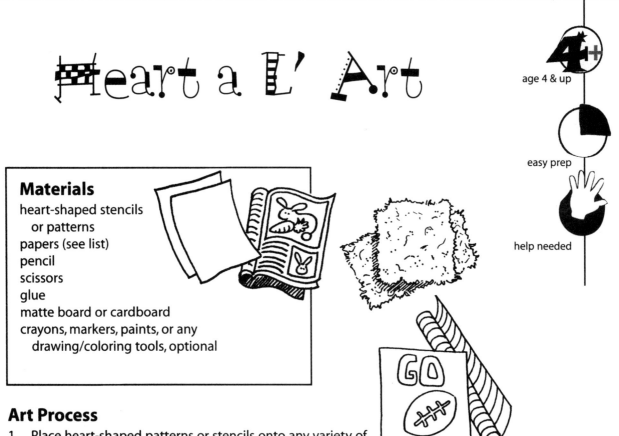

Art Process

1. Place heart-shaped patterns or stencils onto any variety of paper (see list) and trace them. Or, draw hearts free hand.
2. Cut out the heart shapes. Save the heart-shaped holes left in the paper, too.
3. Glue hearts onto a piece of matte board or cardboard in any design or pattern. Fill the matte board with many hearts or just a few (even just one!).
4. If desired, draw or paint additional designs onto the matte board.

Variation

•   Use the hearts to make Valentine cards, mobiles, posters, or wall decorations.

Hint

•   Hearts are often difficult for young artists to draw, so it is fun and practical for them to use stencils and patterns.

Paper Suggestions

book jackets
colored paper
magazine pictures
posters
tissue paper
wrapping paper

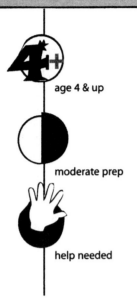

age 4 & up

moderate prep

help needed

Paper Dolls

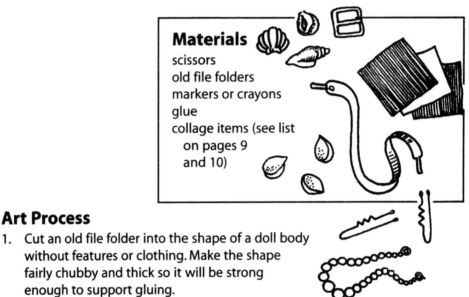

Materials
scissors
old file folders
markers or crayons
glue
collage items (see list
    on pages 9
    and 10)

Art Process
1. Cut an old file folder into the shape of a doll body
   without features or clothing. Make the shape
   fairly chubby and thick so it will be strong
   enough to support gluing.
2. Draw or color on the doll shape.
3. Glue collage items onto the doll shape to make hair, eyes, clothing, jewelry, a
   hat, glasses, or other features.

Variations
- Make characters from a favorite story or play, such as the gingerbread boy, a
  farmer, a farmer's wife, and a fox.
- Turn the paper dolls into puppets. Tape each paper doll to a dowel or stick
  and manipulate them above a partition or curtain.
- Use paper or fabric scraps to make removable clothing for the doll.

Hint
- When moving the wet dolls to a drying area, carry
  them flat. Carrying the doll upright may cause the
  glue and collage items to slide off the doll shape.

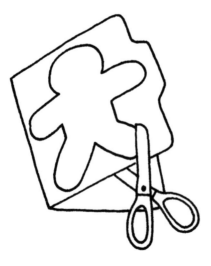

Painted Tissue Collage

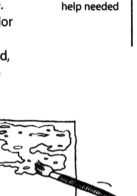

age 4 & up

moderate prep

help needed

Materials

art tissue
tempera paint
wide, soft brush
pencil
large sheet of
   paper
scissors
glue
permanent
   markers, optional

Art Process

1. Place sheets of tissue paper on the worktable.
2. Paint each tissue paper with a contrasting color of tempera paint. (It is not necessary to cover the tissue completely with paint; instead, leave some spaces and brush marks to create texture.)
3. Allow the tissue papers to dry for at least an hour. As the tissue is drying, use a pencil to lightly draw a large, bold picture or design on a sheet of paper. Draw a simple design with very few details (a basic outline).
4. Choose one shape from the drawing. Select a sheet of painted tissue and cut out that same shape from the tissue.

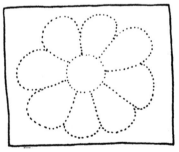

PAINT WITH CONTRASTING COLOR ... IT'S OKAY TO LEAVE SPACES....

5. Glue the tissue piece onto the picture or design. The shape does not have to fit into the drawn space perfectly—use the drawing as a guide only.
6. Select more tissue colors and cut shapes from them to glue onto the drawn pattern.
7. Fill in all of the shapes in the design with the cutout pieces of painted tissue.
8. Allow the entire design to dry.
9. When the design is completely dry, use permanent markers to draw around the shapes. If desired, add more details to the design.

LIGHTLY DRAW A SIMPLE DESIGN...

Hint

- Certain contrasting colors work well together. For example, paint yellow tissue with green paint, red tissue with blue paint, and white tissue with black paint.

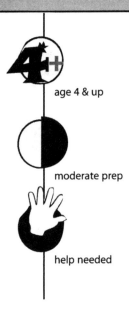

age 4 & up

moderate prep

help needed

My Own Crayon Resist Collage

Art Process

1. Use crayons to draw a pattern of stripes or designs on a piece of paper. Draw over the entire sheet of paper.
2. Make a paint wash by mixing tempera paint and water in a cup until it is thin and watery.
3. Dip a soft paintbrush into the paint wash and "wash" over the crayon patterns. Watch as the crayon patterns "resist" the paint.
4. Allow the design to dry briefly.
5. Cut the designs into a large shape, such as a circle, cloud, flower, or any abstract shape. Save the paper scraps, too.
6. Make additional resist patterns. Cut these into shapes and designs too.
7. Glue the cutout shapes and paper scraps onto a heavy paper background to complete the collage. Overlap the pieces, if desired.

Materials

crayons
paper
tempera paint
water
cups
soft paintbrush
scissors
glue
heavy paper

Variations

- Color patterns such as dots, flowers, plaids, shapes, or any fanciful design.
- Cut crayon patterns into shapes that resemble clothing and hang them on a clothesline with clothespins.
- Create a pattern resist by copying an actual clothing pattern, such as a plaid or striped fabric.

Hint

- A paint wash is a very thin, watery mixture of tempera paint and water. Substitute thinned watercolor paints or food coloring for a paint wash, if desired.

Mosaic Collage

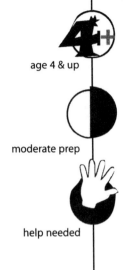

age 4 & up

moderate prep

help needed

Materials
scissors
black or colored contact paper
tape
construction paper
clear contact paper
spoon

Art Process

1. Cut out a 10" x 15" (25 cm x 37 cm) rectangle from a sheet of black or colored contact paper.
2. Peel the covering from the back of the contact paper.
3. Place the contact paper sticky side up on a table. Tape the corners to the table to hold it in place.
4. Cut construction paper into 1" (2 cm) squares. If desired, cut additional shapes such as circles or triangles.
5. Create a mosaic design by sticking the construction paper squares to the contact paper, leaving small spaces between the squares.
6. Cut out a 10" x 15" (25 cm x 37 cm) rectangle from a sheet of clear contact paper.
7. Peel the backing from the clear contact paper and stick it over the completed mosaic design. Smooth out wrinkles, bubbles, and pleats in the contact paper using the back of a spoon.
8. Trim the edges of the mosaic.
9. Use the mosaic as a place mat (wipe it clean with a damp sponge), table art, wall art, or any other decoration.

Variations

*   Create a mat with torn or cut art tissue squares.
*   To display the design on a wall, attach yarn loops to the mat before adding the top layer of contact paper.
*   Use a variety of papers or shapes for the mosaic.

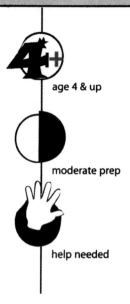

Collage Tree

Art Process

1. Place the base of a bare branch into a large coffee can.
2. Pour pebbles into the can. Then, pour sand on top of the pebbles. The pebbles and sand will keep the branch upright.
3. Glue lightweight collage items (see list) onto the branch. Tie other collage items, such as yarn and twist ties, to the branch too.
4. Fill the branch with collage items as desired.

Materials

branch with no leaves
large coffee can
pebbles
sand
glue
lightweight collage items (see list)
yarn or string

Variation

- Create a "theme tree" for a holiday, season, or celebration. For example, create a birthday theme tree using paper numbers, candles, ribbons, crepe paper, and cutouts from old birthday cards. Or, make a wishing tree by cutting pictures from catalogs of things you would like to give to a loved one.

Lightweight Collage Items

beads
confetti
cotton balls
paper scraps
pieces of foil
string
twist ties
wood shavings
yarn

Fishnet Collage Weave

4+

age 4 & up

moderate prep

help needed

Materials

tacks, pushpins,
  or stapler
fishnet
wall, bulletin board,
  or other flat
  surface
collage materials
  (see list)
scissors

Art Process

1. Tack or staple a fishnet to a wall or other flat surface. Make sure to secure it well.
2. Lace collage materials (see list) through the holes in the fishnet. Be creative. Cross one material over another, knot materials together to make extra long pieces, tie bows and knots, and generally fill the net with color.
3. It may take an artist or group of artists several days to complete the design.
4. Move the completed fishnet to another location and use it as a room divider, window covering, or wall decoration.

Collage Materials

crepe paper
ribbon
rope
strips of fabric
surveyor's tape
thread
yarn

Variations

- Add other collage materials such as beads, buttons, or feathers to the design.
- Use metallic materials, such as aluminum foil and wrapping paper foil, to give the collage a glittery effect.
- Twist plastic bags into ropes for weaving.
- Cut old T-shirts into a spiral, creating a long, continuous strip. Use it for weaving.

Hints

- Substitute an orange, plastic construction fencing net for a fishnet. (Check local lumberyards.)
- To make the collage more mobile and stable, staple the top edge of the fishnet to a strip of wood, and secure the strip of wood to a wall or other flat surface.

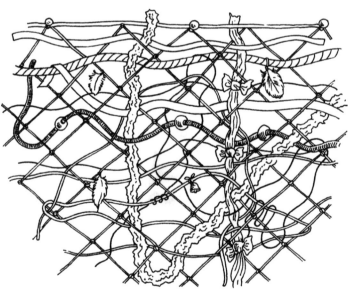

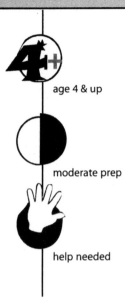

age 4 & up

moderate prep

help needed

Button Sew Collage

Art Process

1. Cut burlap into 2" (5 cm) squares, one for each button.
2. Thread a plastic darning needle with a piece of yarn.
3. Poke the needle and yarn through a square of burlap and then through one of the buttonholes. Pull the yarn all the way through.
4. Push the needle and yarn back through the second buttonhole and the burlap. Tie or sew the yarn to the back of the burlap.
5. Continue sewing buttons onto each burlap square.
6. Put glue or tape on the back of a button square and attach it to a corner of a matte board.
7. Glue or tape another button square next to the first button square.
8. Continue gluing button squares next to each other, completely filling the matte board.
9. Allow the project to dry completely. If desired, frame it with a framing matte.

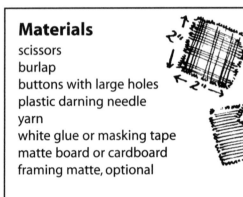

Materials

scissors
burlap
buttons with large holes
plastic darning needle
yarn
white glue or masking tape
matte board or cardboard
framing matte, optional

Variations

- Glue squares in a random design.
- Sew other items with holes to the burlap squares, such as pipe cleaner loops, washers and nuts, beads, small cardboard squares, telephone wire loops, and homemade clay buttons.
- To create contrast, leave a few square spaces on the matte board blank. Then, glue buttons into each blank square. Or, glue brightly colored construction paper to the blank squares.
- Use a fabric with definite squares or circles instead of burlap.
- Instead of using buttons, cut two holes into colorful, heavy paper circles or shapes to resemble two-holed buttons.

Hint

- For very young artists, thread the needle, double the yarn, and knot the loose ends together.

Copier Collage

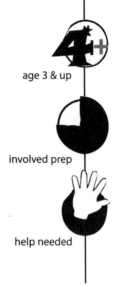
Materials

colored magazine pictures
scissors
copier paper
photocopier
glue
cardboard or heavy paper
crayons, pencils, or markers

Art Process

1. Look through magazines and cut out some of the colored pictures. Large pictures of simple objects work best.
2. Place the pictures on a photocopier and photocopy the pictures in black and white.
3. Cut out the copied pictures.
4. Glue the copied pictures in any design or pattern onto a sheet of cardboard or heavy paper.
5. Let the project dry. Color the pictures with crayon, pencil, or markers.

Variations

- Glue the black and white copies next to the color pictures to make "partner" designs.
- Make photocopies of drawings or photographs for the collage.

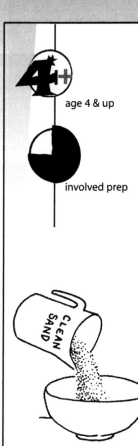

age 4 & up

involved prep

Colored Sand Collage

Art Process

1. Pour the sand into a mixing bowl.
2. Add a few drops of food coloring or powdered tempera paint to color the sand. Stir the mixture with a stick to blend the color evenly.
3. Scoop the sand into a jar and cover it with a lid.
4. Repeat the process to make more colored sand. Make as many colors as desired.
5. Draw on a piece of heavy paper with the glue. Make random designs or a specific picture. (Work on one small area at a time.)
6. Before the glue dries, pour or sprinkle sand over the glue.
7. Draw more glue designs and add more sand, changing colors as desired.

Materials

clean sand
mixing bowls
food coloring or powdered tempera paint,
   several colors
stirring sticks
spoon, scoop, or small shovel
unbreakable transparent jars, with lids
heavy paper or cardboard
white glue, in a squeeze bottle

ADD A FEW DROPS.

STIR !

Variations

- Pour colored sand into Styrofoam grocery trays or shoebox lids. Brush glue onto one side of an index card. (Cut cards into different shapes, too.) Press the glued side of the card into the colored sand, remove it, and let it dry. Create cards for each color of sand and glue them onto a sheet of paper to make one large collage.
- Use spools or small blocks of wood. Dip one end of a spool into the glue and then into the colored sand. Allow it to dry. Sort the colorful spools or blocks on a larger scrap of wood and glue them into place.

DRAW WITH GLUE!

Pumpkin Face Mystery

Materials

scissors
black paper
box or bucket
orange paper
glue or tape

Art Process

1. Cut black paper into strange or realistic shapes that suggest a mouth, eyes, nose, or other facial features. Make the shapes very large or very small.
2. Place the black scrap facial features into a box or bucket.
3. Cut orange paper into circles and ovals ranging from very large to very small.
4. Place a few orange circles or ovals on the floor.
5. Reach into the box and pull out a black feature. Place it on the orange circle and begin building a face for a pumpkin. Design silly, realistic, or scary pumpkin faces.
6. Make several different pumpkin faces. Change the features around to create different expressions and personalities.
7. If desired, tape or glue the features in place and hang the completed pumpkin faces in a window, on a wall, or as a doorway decoration.

Hints

- Some artists will choose to create random designs instead of pumpkin faces. Encourage their creativity and imagination.
- Since artists randomly pull out features from a box, part of this project's fun is the mystery of how the pumpkin face will look.

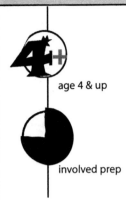

age 4 & up

involved prep

Mystery Collage Planter

Art Process

1. Select a wide, flat planting container. (If using a cardboard box, line it with aluminum foil). Fill the container with potting soil. For better drainage, line the planting container with a layer of gravel before adding the soil.
2. Place the seeds from different seed packets into a bowl and mix them all together. Sprinkle the seeds evenly over the soil in the container. Pat them into the soil.
3. Sprinkle a thin layer of soil over the seeds. Pat the soil again.
4. Thoroughly water the seeds.
5. Wrap a sheet of plastic wrap over the pan (to hold in moisture) and place it in a sunny window. "Vent" the plastic at the corners to allow air to circulate.
6. Water the seeds daily. When the plants begin to sprout, remove the plastic wrap.
7. Keep the soil moist as the plants grow.
8. A wild selection of greenery in a bright collage of shapes and colors will soon fill the pan. Try to identify the plants.
9. When the pan is thick with sprouted plants, transplant selected favorites to an outdoor garden or planting pots.

Materials

flat container, such as a cardboard box, baking pan, or plastic tray with sides at least 2" (5 cm) deep
aluminum foil, if needed
potting soil
gravel, optional
seeds (see list—use at least 4, but no more than 10, kinds)
bowl
water
plastic wrap

Suggested Seeds

chives
green beans
herbs
squash
wildflowers

Variations

- Grow a large mystery garden collage outdoors in a garden.
- Give a mystery potted plant to someone as a gift. Include a card explaining that the plant will be a surprise.

Puzzle Paste

Materials

magazine picture or artist's drawing
scissors
tag board, poster board, or heavy paper
glue

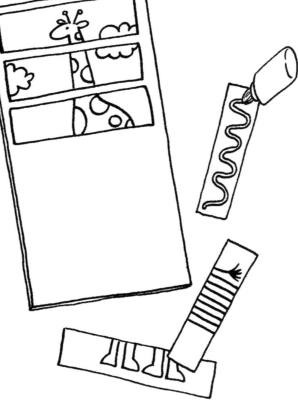

Art Process

1. Choose a magazine picture or an artist's drawing to make a puzzle picture.
2. Cut the picture or drawing into large, simple shapes or strips.
3. Place the pieces of the picture on a tag board or poster board in the same order as the original picture.
4. Pick up a picture piece, place glue on the back of it, and glue it to the tag board.
5. Put glue on a second picture piece and glue it to the tag board, but leave a space between the two pieces.
6. Continue gluing the pieces to the tag board, leaving spaces between each piece.
7. The completed picture will appear to be an optical illusion because of the spaces.

Variation

- Glue a full, uncut picture to a tag board. After it has dried, cut it into strips or large, simple pieces to make a puzzle.

Hint

- If an artist chooses one of his or her own drawings to cut, explain that after the artist cuts it, it cannot be put back together.

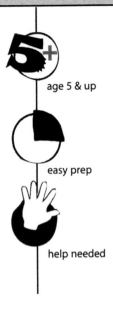

age 5 & up

easy prep

help needed

Mixed-Up Magazine

Materials
scissors
magazine pictures
paste or glue
paper, cardboard,
    box lid, or paper
    plate
pens or crayons

Art Process

1. Cut out many pictures from magazines.
2. Choose one of the magazine pictures. Cut out an important part of the picture, such as the head of a dog, a baby's foot, or a glass of milk.
3. Glue it onto a piece of paper or cardboard.
4. Choose another magazine picture and cut out a part of that picture. Glue it onto the same paper with the first part. The idea is to make a silly picture by combining unrelated parts. For example, place the head of a dog on the body of a boy. Use bananas to make the boy's feet, and so on.

Hints

-   Be creative. Imagine a person with spaghetti for a face and a tree trunk for a body, asleep on a bed of clouds.
-   Young artists find Mixed-Up Magazine incredibly funny. Be prepared for some very silly artists who will make many silly scenes. This project is truly enjoyable!

Magazine Collage Drawing

age 5 & up

easy prep

help needed

Materials

scissors
catalogs, magazines, or photographs
box
glue
drawing paper
colored markers, crayons, or colored pencils

Art Process

1. Tear or cut out simple, uncluttered pictures from magazines or catalogs. Photographs are also great to use—photocopy them or use the original.
2. Save the magazine pictures or photographs in a box.
3. Select a picture with a clear, uncluttered image and glue it onto a piece of paper. For example, use a picture of a woman's smiling face.
4. Draw a picture incorporating the magazine picture into it in some way. Use your imagination! Some examples are:
   - Turn the picture of a woman's face into the strange head of an animal that is part human and part lion or bear.
   - Glue pictures of coins on a drawing to represent flower blossoms in a vase or garden.
   - Draw wings on a cutout horse.
   - Turn a photograph of a flower into a fantastic imaginary bird.
5. Use one or many cutouts for each drawing.

Variations

- Incorporate bright, colorful scraps and shapes of paper into a drawing instead of (or in addition to) magazine pictures.
- Use more than one image to form the central part of the drawing. For example, glue several people or animals into one scene.

Feeling Tree

Art Process

1. Tape a large sheet of paper to a wall. Or, work on an uncovered wall, if desired.
2. Cut brown finger paintings into sections to make a tree trunk and tree branches. Tape the sections to the paper on the wall (or just the wall), forming a large tree.
3. Cut green finger paintings into leaves and tape them to the brown tree.
4. Tape cupcake liners and scraps of colored paper and tissue to the tree to make blossoms.
5. Use collage items, such as straw, grass, or yarn, to make a nest. Tape or glue the nest next to the tree.
6. Cut out birds, eggs, or baby birds from colored paper and tape them into the nest.
7. Cut out other items to add to the tree, such as caterpillars, butterflies, and realistic or imaginary bugs.

Materials

tape
large paper
scissors
finger paintings in brown, green, or any color
cupcake liners
colored paper and tissue
nest collage items, such as straw or grass, newspaper, yarn, or Easter grass
glue

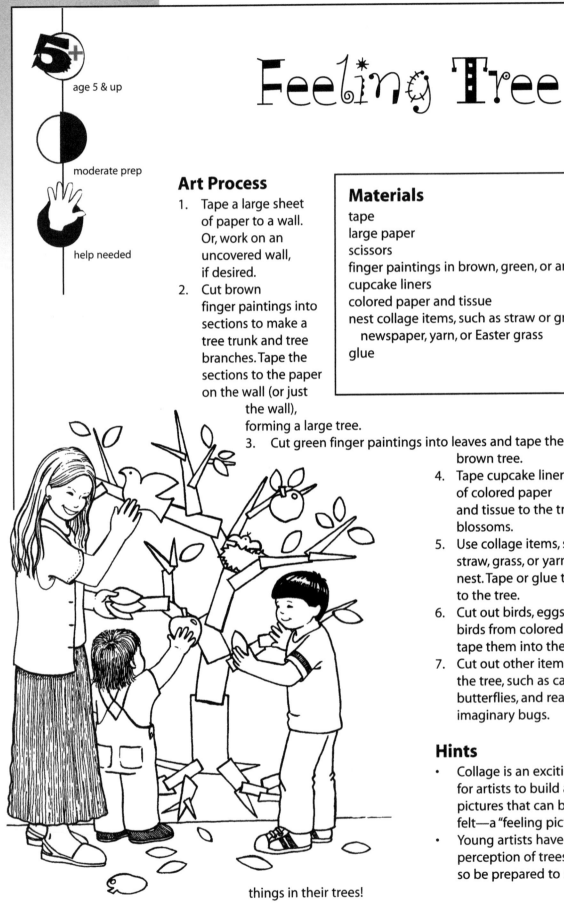

Hints

- Collage is an exciting technique for artists to build and create pictures that can be seen and felt—a "feeling picture."
- Young artists have their own perception of trees and nature, so be prepared to see unusual things in their trees!

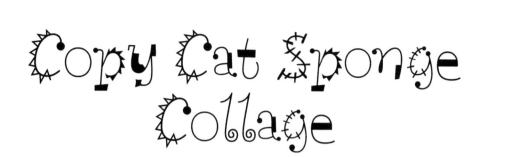

Copy Cat Sponge Collage

Materials

scissors
sponges
paper (see list)
pencil
glue
cardboard or heavy paper
paper towels
water
pans or trays
liquid tempera paints

Art Process

1. Cut sponges into shapes.
2. Place a sponge shape on any paper (see list) and trace it with a pencil. Trace it once or many times. Cut out the paper shapes.
3. Glue the paper shapes onto a piece of cardboard or heavy paper in any pattern or design, overlapping the shapes, if desired.
4. Set the design aside to dry.
5. Make a paint pad for sponge prints. Fold a paper towel into a pad, moisten it with water, and place it into a tray or pan.
6. Pour liquid tempera paint onto the pad. Make a print pad for each color.
7. Moisten the sponge shapes with water.
8. Press a sponge shape into the paint pad, and then press it onto the design next to (or on!) a matching paper shape. The idea is to match similar sponge prints with their paper shape cousins.
9. Continue making sponge prints, matching them with the paper shapes until finished.

Paper Suggestions

construction paper
copier paper
greeting cards
junk mail
magazine pages
tissue paper
wallpaper
wrapping paper

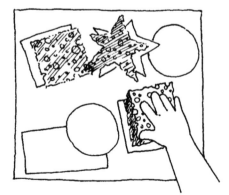

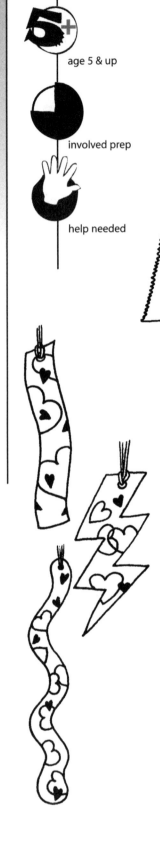

age 5 & up

involved prep

help needed

Heart Flutters

Materials
white glue
dish
water
liquid detergent
wax paper
large paintbrush
scissors
tissue paper
hole punch
yarn or rubber
  bands

Art Process

1. Pour glue into a dish and add water to thin it. Add a few drops of liquid detergent to prevent it from beading.
2. Tear off a large sheet of wax paper. Fold it, and reopen it.
3. Brush thinned white glue over half of the wax paper.
4. Cut or tear tissue paper into heart shapes or other designs.
5. Stick heart shapes or other pieces of torn tissue paper all over the sticky half of the wax paper.
6. Brush more white glue over the hearts or tissue designs. Fold the other half of the wax paper over the design.
7. Allow the design to dry overnight.
8. Cut the dry tissue collage into long, skinny shapes or strips, such as snakes or lightning.
9. Punch a hole into the top of each strip. Loop a rubber band or piece of yarn through the holes. Hang the Heart Flutters from a stick or a hanger. Or, stick pins around a window frame and hang the shapes on the pins.

Variations
- Make bookmarks instead of flutters.
- Frame the tissue collage instead of cutting it into strips.

Hints
- Punch holes at least ⅓" (8 mm) from the flutter's edge to prevent tearing.
- Wet glue looks cloudy, but it will dry clear.

Index

46

Materials Index

50 great ways to explore and create with playdough, tissue mâché, yeast dough, peanut butter dough, and more!

50 great ways to explore and create with lace, string, fabric, glue and other easy-to-find materials!

Clay and Dough
MaryAnn F. Kohl

Encourage children to experience the joy of exploration and discovery with this new series by award-winning author MaryAnn F. Kohl. Excerpted from the national best-seller **Preschool Art,** each book in the series emphasizes the process of art, not the product. **Preschool Art: Clay & Dough** gives you 50 great ways to create with playdough, tissue mâché, yeast dough, peanut butter dough, and more. Make art fun and accessible to children of all ages with these creative, easy-to-do activities!
ISBN 0-87659-250-7 / 16928 / $7.95

Craft and Construction
MaryAnn F. Kohl

Encourage children to experience the joy of exploration and discovery with this new series by award-winning author MaryAnn F. Kohl. Excerpted from the national best-seller **Preschool Art,** each book in the series emphasizes the process of art, not the product. **Preschool Art: Craft & Construction** gives you 50 great ways to create with lace, string, fabric, glue, and other simple materials. Make art fun and accessible to children of all ages with these creative, easy-to-do activities!
ISBN 0-87659-251-5 / 19425 / $7.95

50 great ways to explore and create with chalk, crayons, stencils, textures, and more!

50 great ways to explore and create using baking soda, shoe polish, vegetable dyes, and other surprising materials!

Drawing
MaryAnn F. Kohl

Encourage children to experience the joy of exploration and discovery with this new series by award-winning author MaryAnn F. Kohl. Excerpted from the national best-seller **Preschool Art,** each book in this new series emphasizes the process of art, not the product. **Preschool Art: Drawing** gives you 50 great ways to create with chalk, crayons, stencils, textures, and more! Make art fun and accessible for children of all ages with these creative, easy-to-do activities.
ISBN 0-87659-223-X / 19658 / $7.95

Painting
MaryAnn F. Kohl

Encourage children to experience the joy of exploration and discovery with this new series by award-winning author MaryAnn F. Kohl. Excerpted from the national best-seller **Preschool Art,** each book in the series emphasizes the process of art, not the product.

Preschool Art: Painting brings you 50 great ways to paint using vegetable dyes, baking soda, cornstarch, shoe polish, and other surprising materials. Make art fun and accessible to children of all ages with these creative, easy-to-do activities!
ISBN 0-87659-224-8
13596 / $7.95

 Available at your favorite bookstore, school supply store, or order from Gyphon House at 800.638.0928 or www.gryphonhouse.com.